A Note to Parents and Car

Read-it! Readers are for chil_____ g
road to reading. These beautiful books support both the acquisition of
reading skills and the love of books.

 The PURPLE LEVEL presents basic topics and objects using high
frequency words and simple language patterns.

 The RED LEVEL presents familiar topics using common words
and repeating sentence patterns.

 The BLUE LEVEL presents new ideas using a larger vocabulary
and varied sentence structure.

 The YELLOW LEVEL presents more challenging ideas, a broad
vocabulary, and wide variety in sentence structure.

 The GREEN LEVEL presents more complex ideas, an extended
vocabulary range, and expanded language structures.

 The ORANGE LEVEL presents a wide range of ideas and concepts
using challenging vocabulary and complex language structures.

When sharing a book with your child, read in short stretches, pausing
often to talk about the pictures. Have your child turn the pages and
point to the pictures and familiar words. And be sure to reread favorite
stories or parts of stories.

There is no right or wrong way to share books with children. Find time
to read with your child, and pass on the legacy of literacy.

Adria F. Klein, Ph.D.
Professor Emeritus
California State University
San Bernardino, California

Editor: Patricia Stockland
Page Production: Melissa Kes/JoAnne Nelson/Tracy Davies
Art Director: Keith Griffin
Managing Editor: Catherine Neitge
The illustrations in this book were done in acrylic.

Picture Window Books
151 Good Counsel Drive
P.O. Box 669
Mankato, MN 56002-0669
877-845-8392
www.picturewindowbooks.com

Printed in the United States of America in North Mankato, Minnesota.
072009
0005334

Library of Congress Cataloging-in-Publication Data
Jones, Christianne C.
Stone soup / by Christianne C. Jones ; illustrated by Micah Chambers-Goldberg.
p. cm. — (Read-it! readers folk tales)
Summary: Retells the classic tale in which a poor but clever traveler finds a way to
get the townspeople to share their food with him.
ISBN 978-1-4048-0978-9 (library binding)
ISBN 978-1-4048-1256-7 (softcover)
ISBN 978-1-4048-1256-7 (softcover)
[1. Folklore.] I. Chambers-Goldberg, Micah, ill. II. Title. III. Series.

PZ8.1.J646St 2005
398.2—dc22   2004018421

Stone Soup

By Christianne C. Jones
Illustrated by Micah Chambers-Goldberg

Special thanks to our advisers for their expertise:

Adria F. Klein, Ph.D.
Professor Emeritus, California State University
San Bernardino, California

Susan Kesselring, M.A.
Literacy Educator
Rosemount-Apple Valley-Eagan (Minnesota) School District

Picture Window Books
Minneapolis, Minnesota

After walking all day, a poor traveler came to a small town.

He was tired and hungry.

The traveler stopped at the
first house.

A strange old couple lived there.

8

"I've been traveling all day, and I am very hungry. Do you have any food to spare?" asked the traveler.

"We do not have any food to spare. Try the next house," the old couple said.

So, the traveler walked to the next house.

He tried the next house and the house
after that. He knocked on every door
in town.

Not one person was willing to give him something to eat.

The traveler did not give up. He would find a way to get some food.

In fact, he had a grand idea!

The traveler yelled, "If no one has food to spare, I will make stone soup for everyone. All I need is a big pot and some water to get started."

An old man brought out a large pot.

A young boy fetched some water.

A fire was started, and the water began to boil.

"Now I need a big stone," the traveler said, as the townspeople began to gather.

A young girl ran over with a huge stone. Into the pot it went.

The traveler said, "This looks good. But it would be better if we had some carrots."

A young woman brought some carrots. Into the pot they went.

"Perfect," said the traveler. "If only

we had some potatoes, too."

A strong man hauled in a bag of potatoes. They all went into the pot.

One by one, the townspeople brought vegetables. Onions! Celery! Peas! Corn! Beans!

When the soup was done, the townspeople could not believe their eyes!

The soup that started with one stone had become a huge feast for the entire town.

And the townspeople ate until they were full, even the poor traveler.

More *Read-it!* Readers

Bright pictures and fun stories help you practice your reading skills. Look for more books at your level.

Beauty and the Beast	*Sleeping Beauty*
The Brave Little Tailor	*Snow White*
The Frog Prince	*The Steadfast Tin Soldier*
Hansel and Gretel	*Thumbelina*
The Little Mermaid	*Tom Thumb*
Puss in Boots	*The Ugly Duckling*
Rapunzel	*The Wolf and the Seven Little Kids*

On the Web

FactHound offers a safe, fun way to find Web sites related to topics in this book. All of the sites on FactHound have been researched by our staff.

1. Visit *www.facthound.com*

2. Type in this special code:
   1404809783

3. Click on the FETCH IT button.

Your trusty FactHound will fetch the best sites for you!
A complete list of *Read-it!* Readers is available on our Web site:
www.picturewindowbooks.com